'M NOT DOING THAT ANYMORE

DIY BOUNDARIES MANIFESTO

1. WRITE DOWN AN ANSWER FOR EVERY BLANK IN THIS BOOK.

Some of them, you've known all along. Some of them will surprise you. Some of them will pour right out before you have the chance to think them through.

THERE'S MORE THAN

2. *DON'T* WRITE DOWN YOUR ANSWERS.

Instead, return to these blanks as often as you like.

Pay attention to your answers. Notice how and when they change... how they pull you toward growth. How they do not stay the same.

3. READ THIS LIKE A BOOK.

Keep it in one piece. Leave it on your coffee table, put it by your bed. Leaf through it as often as you need.

ONE WAY TO DO THIS.

4. TEAR THE PAGES OUT.

Tape them to your walls. Frame them on your desk. Live with the questions they ask.

Let your truth speak here, and shape everything that comes next.

STARTING NOW,
I RESPECT MYSELF
WAY TOO
MUCH
TO CONTINUE

....

Just because I can ______________ doesn't mean I have to.

It turns out I'm done pretending to ______________________.

I will
no longer

just to make
other people
comfortable.

LESS
LESS
LESS
LESS
LESS
LESS
LESS

I WANT TO HOLD MYSELF TO THIS.

I don't need to

....

by myself.

This is permission to ask for help.

I WILL BE AS

TO MYSELF
AS I AM TO
EVERYONE
ELSE.

THINGS WILL BE ALRIGHT IF I ....

TODAY, I WILL TRUST THIS.

IT'S OK
TO NEED

I NEED.

I AM OFFICIALLY INVITING

MORE

____

INTO MY LIFE.

IT'S TIME FOR ME TO TAKE

____

SERIOUSLY, EVEN IF IT'S UNCOMFORTABLE.

(MAYBE ESPECIALLY.)

I WOULD RATHER BE

myself

THAN

....

I WOULD
RATHER BE
THAN
NICE.

MY

IS MY POWER.

AND I KNOW THIS.

IN MY TIME ON EARTH, I WANT TO

TODAY, I PRIORITIZE

OVER

IS WORTH THE

☑ WORK,

☑ TIME,

AND

☑ RISK.

FROM NOW ON,

IS A REQUIREMENT FOR ME.

COMPENDIUM®
live inspired

An imprint of the Crown Publishing Group
A division of Penguin Random House LLC
1745 Broadway, New York, NY 10019
live-inspired.com | penguinrandomhouse.com

ISBN: 978-1-957891-74-3

Writer: M.H. Clark
Illustrator: Jessica Phoenix
Editor: Bailey Vega
Production Manager: Shannon Lery

1st printing. Manufactured in China with soy inks on FSC®-Mix certified paper.

The authorized representative in the EU for product safety and compliance is Penguin Random House Ireland, Morrison Chambers, 32 Nassau Street, Dublin D02 YH68, Ireland, https://eu-contact.penguin.ie.

Create meaningful moments with gifts that inspire.

CONNECT WITH US
live-inspired.com | sayhello@compendiuminc.com

@compendiumliveinspired
#compendiumliveinspired